Denis Galanin

THE AMAZING WORLD OF VIDEO GAME DEVELOPMENT

FAMILIUS

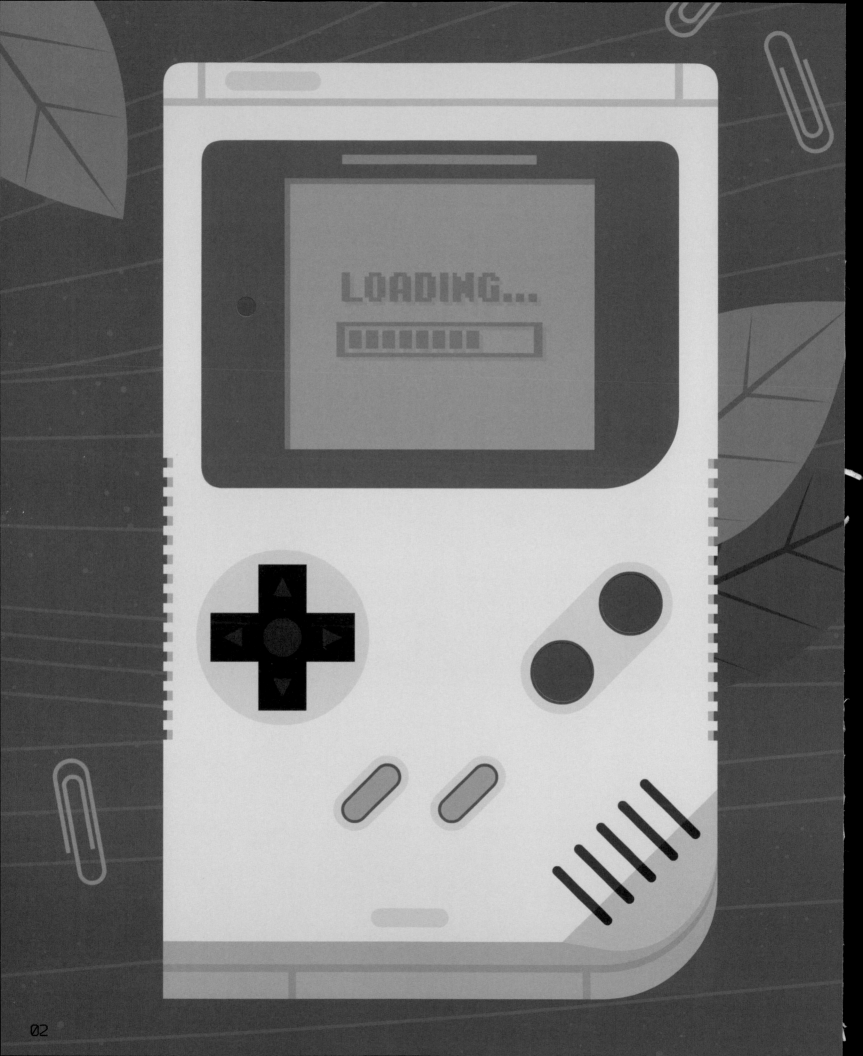

CONTENTS

INTRODUCTION

For many years, children and adults have enjoyed playing video games. But video games are still a new form of entertainment.

Although the first video games appeared in the 1940s, only in the 80s did they take the form we see today.

BUT HAVE YOU EVER WONDERED HOW VIDEO GAMES ARE MADE?

Before answering this question, let's check this list of the things that are needed to create a video game.

Interesting Idea   [x]

Electronic Computer   [x]

Positive Attitude   [x]

Passion and Enthusiasm   [x]

But what else is needed? A team to create the video game!

GAME DESIGNER

In game development, the first person who is needed is a Game Designer.

The Game Designer creates the game's rules and levels, writes its scripts, and adjusts the strengths, weaknesses, and other features of its characters.

It is helpful for a Game Designer to be well versed not only in board games, sports, and video games, but also in mathematics, psychology, storytelling, directing, and even architecture.

GAME PROGRAMMER

The Game Programmer is responsible for implementing all the technical tasks in video game development. Being well versed in various programming languages, the Game Programmer implements the most daring ideas of the Game Designer and Game Artist while also making sure that there aren't any serious errors in the video game.

The Game Programmer's main task is to make sure the Game Engine works as it should.

1101001 1100100 1100100
1110001 1100100

```
C:\>_
```

The Game Engine is the heart of a video game. It is a computer program, which is a collection of various tools that enable the video game to work as it is designed to.

GAME ARTIST

The Game Artist designs and creates all the video game's visuals, from simple sketches to three-dimensional models.

Concept art, textures, backgrounds, animations, user interface, special effects, and any other elements related to the visual design of the video game are all part of the work of the Game Artist.

The Game Artist tries to make the visual style of the video game unique and memorable, because a gamer's first impression of the game is formed from the screenshots and videos they see and watch to learn about the game before they even play it.

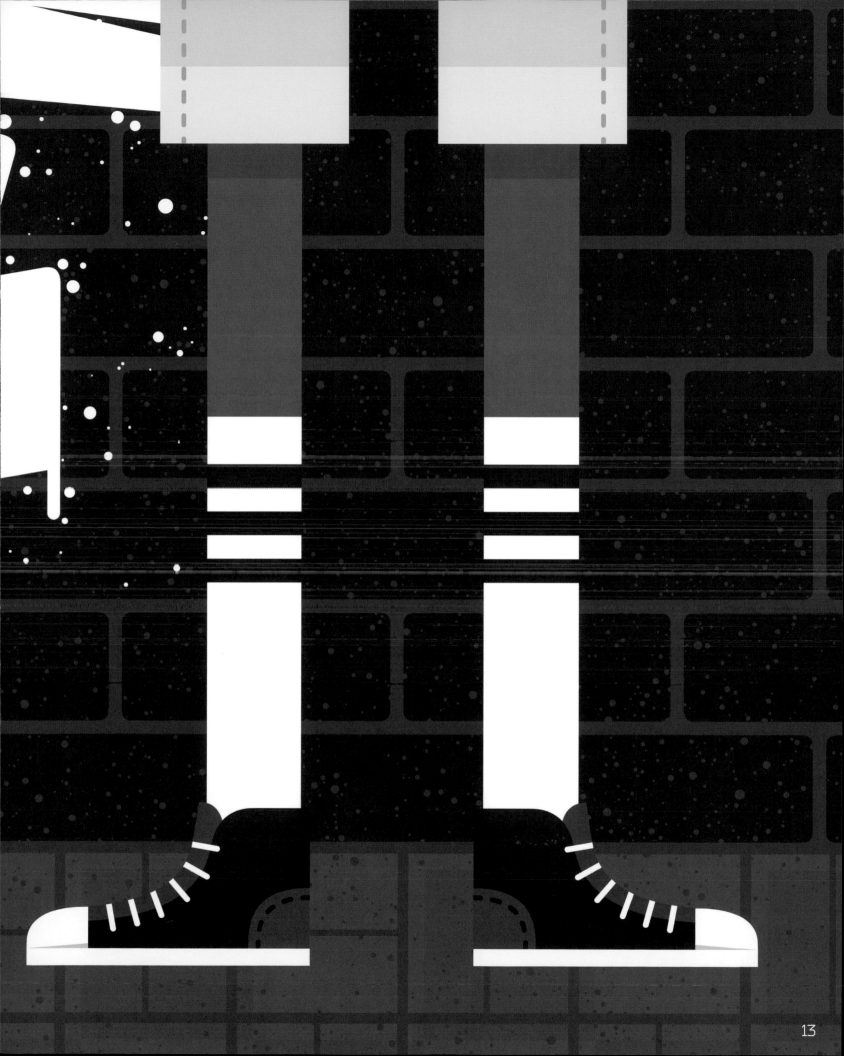

COMPOSER AND SOUND DESIGNER

Sounds and music are very important components of the video game because they shape its mood and atmosphere.

The Composer composes the music for the video game. Due to the variety of game genres and themes, the Composer must be equally well versed in both classical overtures and symphonies, and the most modern musical experiments.

Unlike the Composer, the Sound Designer does not create music, but fills a video game with a variety of sound effects and noises for different features of the game.

GAME TESTER

Not all roles in the development team are creative or directly related to developing the game.

At its core, a video game is a large computer program. And in any computer program created by a person, errors can happen that cause the game to not work properly, whether in the game's code, or its various parameters, character animations, or images. Here, the Game Tester comes to the rescue to find and record any errors in the game so they can be fixed.

Unlike other team members, the Game Tester doesn't need to have any specific knowledge or skills.

GAME DIRECTOR

Just as every book has an Author and every ship has a Captain, every video game has a Game Director.

The Game Director is the most important person on the video game development team. The Game Director controls not only the creative component of the video game but also all other aspects of the game's development.

Ultimately, it is the Game Director who decides what the game should look like, which elements should be removed from it, and which should be added or changed.

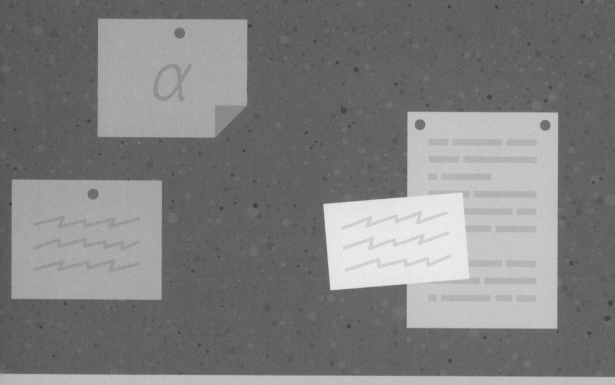

In other words, the Game Director performs functions similar to those of a Director of plays and movies.

TEAM SIZE

But how many people should be on a development team? There is no definite answer. Most often, it depends on the size of the video game.

Dozens or even hundreds of people take part in the creation of a large and complex game, each of whom is responsible for their own small part of the video game.

However, when creating a small video game, there isn't any point in a large development team, so only a few people participate and combine all the necessary roles.

And sometimes one person is able to replace an entire team and be the Game Designer, Game Artist, Game Programmer, and Composer all at the same time.

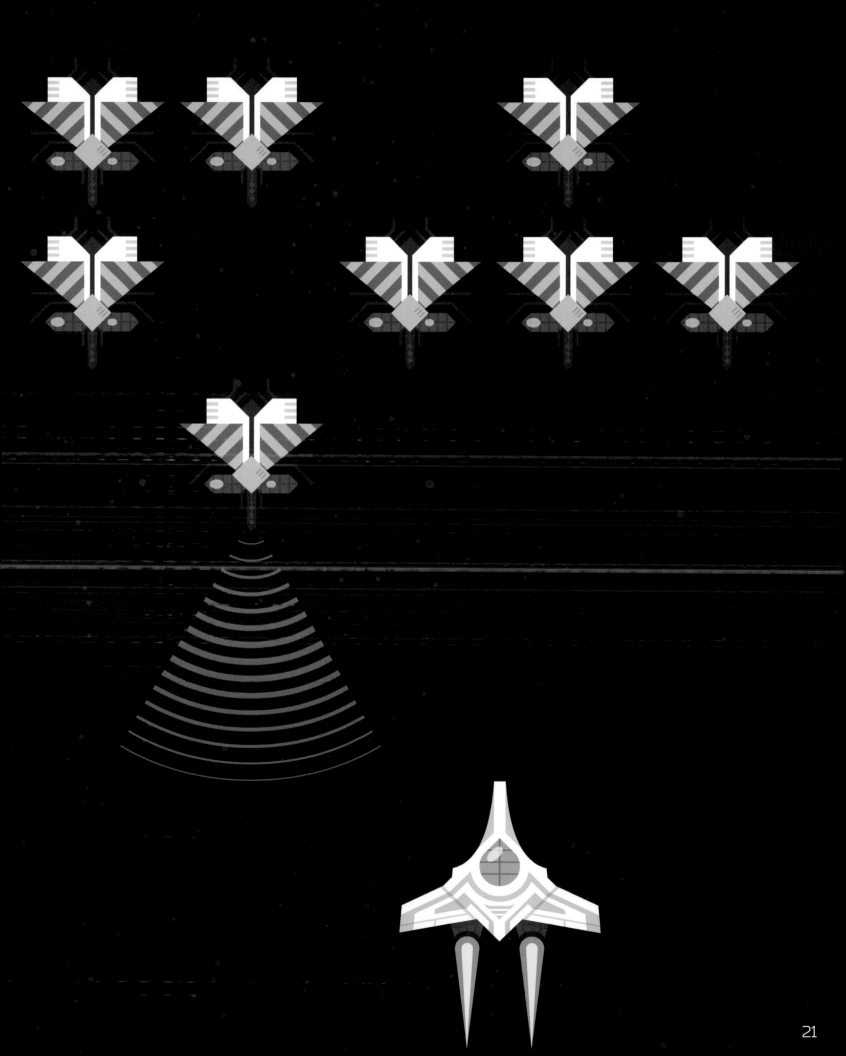

STAGES OF VIDEO GAME DEVELOPMENT

IDEA

A video game starts with an idea. But at the initial stage, this idea is usually too large and complex, overflowing with unnecessary details.

PRE-PRODUCTION

At this stage, the idea from someone's fantasy turns into something real. It is here that the "skeleton," or basic structure of the future video game, is formed.

Now that the team is assembled, they can proceed directly to the development of the video game. The video game development process can be roughly divided into four main stages.

PRODUCTION

During this stage, the video game is constantly changing, filling with more and more important details until it eventually begins to take its final form.

RELEASE

The long-awaited moment when the development is fully completed. But by the time of release, the video game may be very different from its original idea.

WHY AND FOR WHOM?

Before starting to turn an idea into a video game, the development team needs to answer this question:
Why and for whom is this video game being created?

WHY IS A VIDEO GAME CREATED?

There are many different goals for creating a video game: to earn recognition and receive awards, to achieve commercial success, or just to have fun with the developmental process.

The development team is free to choose any goal for themselves, so long as they clearly state their goal and stick to it throughout the development process.

FOR WHOM IS THIS VIDEO GAME BEING CREATED?

Usually, a video game is always liked by the development team, their relatives, and friends. But what will other people think of this video game? Will they find it interesting, and would they want to play it?

To answer this, the team imagines the kind of player for whom the video game is being created to make sure it will be a game they will enjoy.

After the development team has discussed and approved the idea of a video game, Pre-production begins.

The Game Designer works out the idea, identifies key game mechanics, determines the main features of the game, and chooses the most suitable genre, setting, and atmosphere.

All of this information is recorded in the Game Design Document. The Game Programmer evaluates how difficult the video game will be to create and puts together the Game Prototype.

The Game Artist draws the first sketches of the environment, characters, and other game objects.

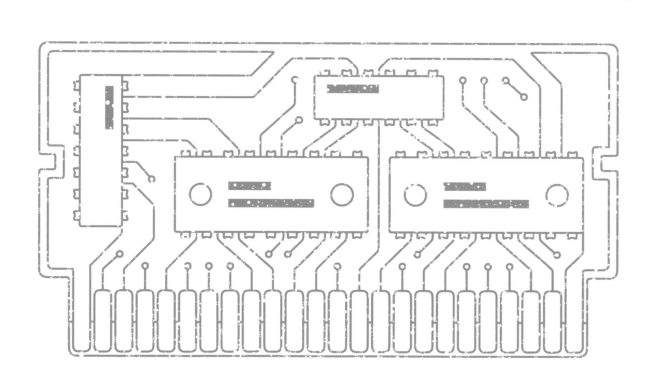

GAME DESIGN DOCUMENT

This is a detailed description of all the details and elements of the video game.

During the development process, the Game Designer adds new information about the game to the Game Design Document. But the video game's basic rules are set in the Game Design Document during Pre-production.

GAME PROTOTYPE

This is the very first version of the video game, which still needs more work to be its best, but already gives a clear idea of what the game will become.

The goal of Pre-production is to produce a first draft of the Game Design Document, an interesting Game Prototype, and a detailed Development Plan.

ODUCTIO

When all tasks are defined and the video game's elements are detailed, the team can start Production. This is the longest and most important stage, which can last several years. Therefore, it is very important that the team maintains interest in the game throughout the development period.

During Production, the video game's code, graphics, levels, sounds, music, texts, and more are created.

During the development process, the game is constantly changing because some ideas are rejected when they don't turn out to be interesting or even successful when implemented.

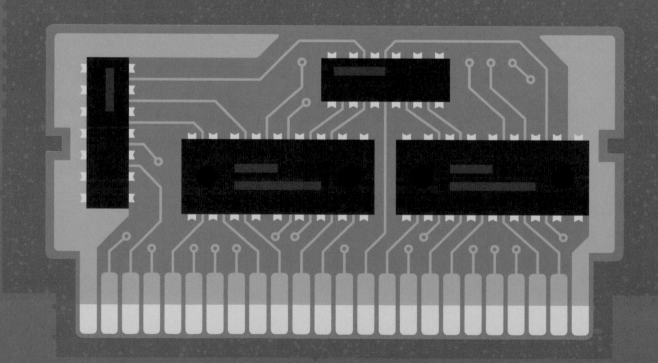

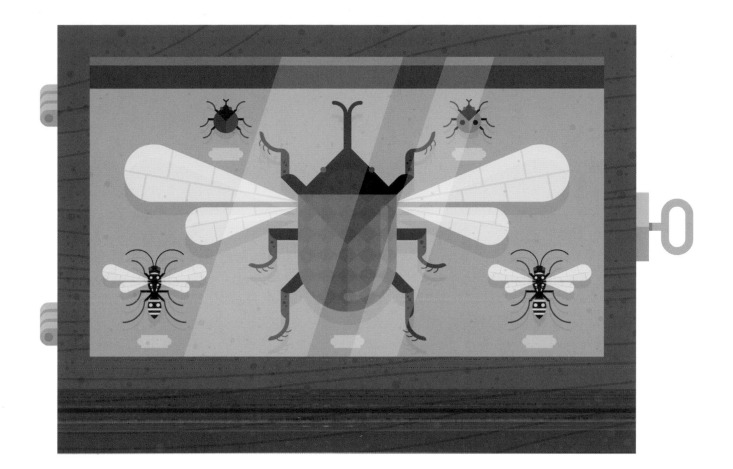

BUGS

Any serious malfunction in a video game is called a Bug.

Sometimes the effect of the Bug surprisingly makes the game better and the Game Developer decides to keep it in the game. As a result, a Bug can become one of the game's main features.

Video game development is a creative process, so each team has its own development culture and creates the rules that are the most comfortable and effective for it. As a result, there are no uniform or universal rules for developing video games.

RELEASE

Finally, the day comes when the team realizes that the video game is complete.

All the serious bugs have been fixed and the final polishing and adjustment of the game's elements has been done, which means that it is time to release the video game into the world of other video games.

THE END?

No, not yet. After the video game's Release, its real life is just beginning!

 NOTES

PAGE 02
Game Boy, 1989. A handheld game console with swappable game cartridges.

PAGE 04
Game & Watch, 1980. A series of handheld electronic gaming devices.

PAGE 06
Macintosh 128K, 1984. A personal computer.

PAGE 17
Virtual Boy, 1995. A portable video game console with stereoscopic display.

PAGE 28
Famicom cartridge board, 1983.

PAGE 30
Famicom game cartridge, 1983.

Published by Familius LLC, www.familius.com
PO Box 1249, Reedley, CA 93654

Familius books are available at special discounts for bulk purchases, whether for sales promotions or for family or corporate use. For more information, contact Familius Sales at orders@familius.com.

Library of Congress Control Number: 2022934508

Print ISBN 9781641707497
Ebook ISBN 9781641707695
ISBN KF 9781641707794
ISBN FE 9781641707893

Printed in China

Edited by Erin Lund
Cover and book design by Denis Galanin

10 9 8 7 6 5 4 3 2 1
First Edition